The Messenger's Guide to Creating a Website

A Self-Study Course to Help Transformational Leaders Plan & Map Out the Key Pages of their Website

Terikka Faciane, M.Ed.
Messenger Midwife

www.yourtribeiswaiting.com
ISBN-13: 978-1533625366
ISBN-10: 1533625360

Hello Messenger,

Welcome to *The Messenger's Guide to Creating a Website Self-Study Course!* I am so excited to be on this journey with you! As a midwife to Messengers, my sole aim is to help you ***clarify, refine, and birth*** your God-given message so you can begin effectively reaching your tribe.

It is not enough to have a message, we must have various platforms to share that message, and an online presence (i.e. a website) is a non-negotiable. Your tribe needs to know where to find you, who you are, what transformation you offer, and more specifically, how you can help them.

This *Self-Study Course* was designed with the Messenger (i.e. Transformational Leader) in mind. This course will guide you through identifying the key pages you need to build an effective website and the content you will need to create to communicate clearly to your tribe.

Your content and design can make the difference between your tribe understanding you and your message or missing the importance of your message altogether. We do not want them to miss the transformation you have to offer.

Are you ready to get clear? It's time to make your presence and message known!

Let's begin, your tribe is waiting for you!

Your Course Facilitator & Fellow Messenger,

Terikka Faciane, M.Ed.
Messenger Midwife
www.yourtribeiswaiting.com

TABLE OF CONTENTS

YOUR LIFE
IS YOUR
MESSAGE
TO THE
WORLD.
MAKE SURE
IT'S
INSPIRING.

Overview of Our Learning Objectives

By the time you complete this self-study course, you will be able to:

➢ Identify the key pages you need to build an effective website for tribe member engagement
➢ Discover the most important pieces to incorporate into your website's Home Page
➢ Create an About Us page that tells your story and tells about the transformation you offer
➢ Engage potential tribe members so that they want to know more
➢ Discover the importance of the Start Here or Welcome Page and the advantages it gives your website's engagement with potential tribe members
➢ Recognize the value of a well-designed Blog page that will help you build influence and get your website seen
➢ Explore the other web pages you need that are both essential and specific to your ministry/business, along with tips for what to include on each of those pages
➢ Implement best practices for creating website content that produces an interactive and compelling website for maximum engagement
➢ Draft a personalized action plan for revising your current web pages and adding additional content if necessary.

Now go grab the essentials and let's dig in!

Introduction – Key Pages for Your Website

When a potential tribe member arrives at your website, what do you want them to do? Do you want them to join your mailing list? Or browse your course offerings and sign up for your signature program? Maybe you want visitors to your website to simply enjoy your blog posts and other content. Or maybe, your website is aimed at gaining exposure so you can expand your reach.

A good way to approach website design is to realize that there are no "good" or "bad" websites; there are simply those that are effective or ineffective in reaching that stated end goal. How do you decide what pages go on your website and how it's arranged? Start with the end goal in mind and determine which design elements will best help you reach that end.

This course teaches you how to create the most critical pages on your website that will lead your visitors to take the action that you want them to take.

Before you start designing your website, you need to clarify these key points:

➢ Who are you and what do you do? How will you communicate this to potential tribe members who come to your website?
➢ What are you offering? (You could be offering products, services, information, etc.)
➢ What call-to-action do you want to create for your potential tribe members, based on your offering?
➢ Do you want them to make a purchase or join a mailing list? Would you like them to become part of your community or become aware of your brand or organization?
➢ Where did the visitor come from? Did they come from an email, a blog, a social media link, or a search engine? This determines their mindset when they reach your page.
➢ Now that they're here, what will keep them here?
➢ What does the visitor need and what is the visitor looking for? You have to put this on the right page in order for them to find it.

You will really need to reflect on and have some clarity around these questions, but know that one goal will always be to capture their email address so you can have permission to stay in touch with them.

You may choose to organize your website by segmenting it to address the various phases your tribe members may find themselves in on their journey. You can organize it by those who are new to your topic, those who are aware but have gotten discouraged along the way... You could organize it for individuals, groups, or organizations. The key is to organize your website in such a way that the visitor knows what is for whom.

With all of the above in mind, you have to prioritize your web content and then decide what goes on which page. This is how you maximize your web content and ultimately your reach.

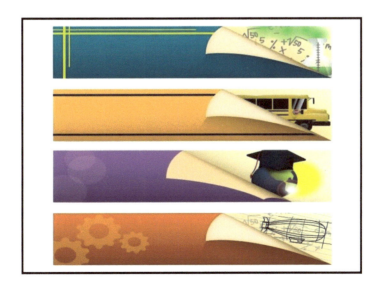

In this self-study course, you will learn how to do that for the four most important pages that every successful website needs. The four key pages are:

1. **Home Page:** Your home page paints your ministry, coaching practice, or business in broad strokes. It tells your story in a very concise way, explaining at-a-glance what you do, who you do it for and how you do it. The home page directs the potential tribe member to all of your website's other pages. It serves as a portal to everything else your site has to offer, as well as other sites you may maintain as well.

2. **About Us:** Your About Us page is where your potential tribe member gets to know more about your message and business, including its history, the reason behind it, your mission and vision, testimonials from others you have served, and so on. In other words, it offers a closer look at your ministry/business, not its offerings or other content. The About Us page may also link to other sites, social media, etc.

3. **Start Here Page:** The Start Here Page is a place to start in exploring your website. Where is your potential tribe member coming from? What do they expect to find when they land at your site? Present to them here the first information they need to know about you and your site in order to find what they need. This is their first step toward the eventual end goal you want them to take. It leads them to take the second step.

4. **Blog Page:** Your blog is your online journal. It is frequently updated with news and helpful information. Your most recent posts are first, and there is an archive that allows visitors to explore earlier posts. They can also search for specific information they want using keywords.

There are other important pages, like your 404 page, a Contact Us page, and more, which we'll cover later in the course.

You may also need to add other pages, depending on the goal of your site. For example, if your website's goal is to enroll students in your courses, you need an online course catalog and shopping cart. You may want to have a FAQ page, and there may be sign-up pages for email lists or membership sites.

Determining the Key Pages for Your Website

1. List the primary goals of your website.

	Goals	Notes
1		
2		
3		

Who are you? What is your message? Who is your Ideal Tribe Member? *(See Appendix to clarify your Ideal Tribe Member)*

What awareness and transformation opportunities do you offer?

2. Write an overview of the information you feel is needed in your website content. What does your tribe member need? What are they looking for? How does your transformative message fill that need?

What does your tribe member need?

What are they looking for?

How do you fill that need?

Other key points

Create an Impeccable Home Page

Your website's Home Page is its main page. It's important to tell potential tribe members visiting your website who you are, who you serve, what you do, and what you have to offer. This is the page most will visit first, so it's very important that it's clear and effective. It should address your potential tribe members' questions and needs, and show them where to go for the solution they're looking for.

To design your Home Page, start with the goal you have in mind for it. Put yourself in your potential tribe members' shoes. You've come here from a link in an article, advertisement, social media post, referral etc. What's the next thing on your mind? You just saw a Facebook ad, an informative video or read an article; you clicked through and now you're here.

Some of the questions brimming in your mind might include:

➢ Who is this?
➢ What do they do?
➢ Who did they serve?
➢ What makes them different?
➢ What else do they have to offer?

The purpose of the content here is to answer these basic questions and steer the potential tribe member in the direction that you want them to go in. Start by saying clearly who you are and what you do.

For example, you posted a video online sharing one of your coaching programs and your website sells this program. When a person comes to your site, your Home Page should tell them:

➢ We're an X Messenger that sells programs for X people wanting to experience transformation in doing X.
➢ Yes, we have the program you saw in the video.
➢ We offer the most impactful range of coaching programs for those desiring clarity or transformation in this area.
➢ Come and visit our online course catalog; there is plenty of information and the registration process is easy.

The Elements of a Good Home Page

A good Home Page is compelling. It makes a potential tribe member want to stay and interact with it. It does this by speaking clearly to the potential tribe members' needs and expectations (what they expect when they click the link and come to your site). It says this clearly in the title or headline. It also lets the potential tribe member know that yes, this is the right place (for example, it has the same logo as the video that links back to it).

A good Home Page is well-organized and pleasing to the eye. It is easy to take everything in at a glance. It's good to have different media and features, but they shouldn't be distracting. Your Home Page shouldn't be cluttered. Your message to the potential tribe member should be at the forefront.

Being well-organized also means that navigation is clear. Your Home Page explains all of the website's other pages and it's easy for the potential tribe member to understand how to get to them.

Your Home Page should be dynamic. Consider including updates, news, announcements, and the latest changes.

Fresh content gives visitors a reason to bookmark and come back. It also offers SEO benefits. The search engines favor sites with changing content. Change content on your Home Page according to potential tribe members' needs. For example, if there's a question many potential tribe members have been asking you recently, provide an answer on your Home Page.

The Essential Components of a Good Home Page

Your Home Page should include:

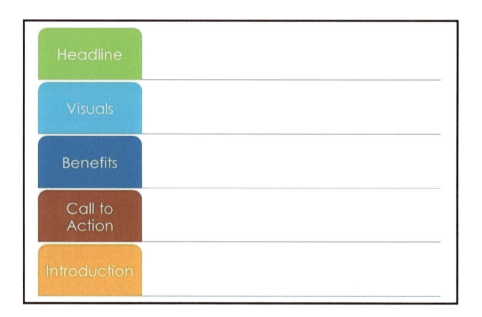

> ➢ **A headline that says who you are**. This one line should explain succinctly and clearly who you are and what you do. This is the first part of the page the viewer will see, so it's important for it to speak to their needs.

> ➢ **Visuals**. It's good to include at least one visual that relates to your business or services. Again, make sure this matches the expectations of the potential tribe member to your site.

- ➤ **A bullet-point list of benefits for the visitor**. These should explain the positive improvement in the potential tribe member's life that your website and/or its services provide. For example:
    - ○ "This is the most comprehensive course for getting unstuck and living a life with purpose."
    - ○ "We provide all of the tips and courses you need for making lasting change, in one place."
    - ○ "Our signature programs and accountability groups can help you find the support and motivation you need today."

- ➤ **Call to action**. The call to action tells the potential tribe member what they must do in order to receive the listed benefits. It includes an action word and a time phrase to give it urgency – "Get started today."

- ➤ **Introduction to the other pages on your site...** and what your visitor will find when they go there. Explain how each page will help them by speaking to their needs with phrases like:
    - ○ "Need help with...?"
    - ○ "Want to see what others have to say about us?"
    - ○ "See what's new on our blog..."

Additional Optional Components for Your Home Page

Content Offer

You may offer some kind of content on your Home Page. For example, you might have an information product for download. Some websites put a freebie on their Home Page in order to sign up visitors to their email list. The Home Page is often the most visited page, so it's a good opportunity. The content here could be an eBook, a podcast, templates or tools, a resource list, exclusive membership, or anything else.

Social Proof & Testimonials

Social proof means content such as testimonials or reviews that show what other people, such as former customers or clients, have to say about your website or company. It helps to build trust with the new visitor. It also shows that your offer is worth checking out, as it helped other people achieve a similar goal to yours. One way to do this is to include recent social media activity which shows your social media followers actively engaging with you.

Content for Your Home Page

The content on your Home Page should be brief. Remember, this is just a chance for the visitor to take in what you do at a glance. More in-depth content will go elsewhere on your website.

Make your content here personal. The goal is to connect with your reader. Write from their perspective and use a tone that's conversational, friendly, and easy to understand.

Break up text into small paragraphs with sub-headers for each. Make it easy to skim your Home Page so that the potential tribe member can get specific questions answered and find the information that they're searching for.

Use keywords in a natural way so that you'll get more search engine traffic. A keyword is a single word or short phrase that's related to your message or business. These are the terms people are searching for on search engines like Google. If you're not sure which keywords to use, use a tool like Google's free keyword research tool to get ideas.

Finally, always proofread all content for your Home Page and every page of your site. For your Home Page, this is the visitor's first impression of you and your business. Don't turn them away with typos or spelling mistakes. Make sure it is well written.

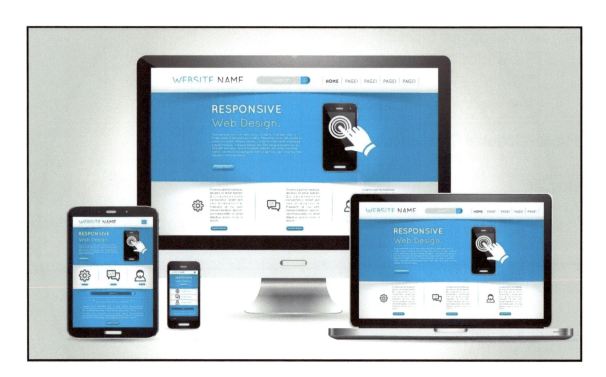

Here are a few examples of clean, streamlined Home Pages:

(For a closer look visit **www.yourtribeiswaiting.com**)

(For a closer look visit **www.michaelhyatt.com**)

Creating an Impeccable Home Page

1. Examine your current Home Page and what it should be saying about your message and services. Based on the module, what is missing, or needs to be added or enhanced?

Is it compelling?	
Is it well-organized?	
How clear is the navigation?	
Is it dynamic?	
Does it have:	
A headline that says who you are?	
Visuals?	
A bullet-point list of benefits?	
A call to action?	
Introduction to other pages?	
A content offer?	
Social proof/Testimonials?	

2. Based on your analysis in step one, draft content for your Home Page using the key points from the module and your message's keywords and keyword phrases.

Design Your Awesome About Us Page

The About Page of your website further engages potential tribe members and starts building a trusting relationship with them. They come here for a variety of different reasons. They want to know more about you, your message, and your business and they want to know that you're legitimate. They're looking for similar values.

Many people haphazardly put together their About Page, thinking it's not as important as their Home Page or content pages. But along with the Home Page, this is often the most-visited page of a website.

Creating Your About Page Content

The purpose of your About Page is to tell the visitor about you. So, it should be personal. Use this as a chance to tell your story. Tell your story but don't get into the specifics or benefits of your products or services (that will be done on your Products and Services pages).

For example, your About Page could tell the visitor about the birth of your business. This includes not only when and where your vision started, but also why it started. This is a great opportunity to communicate your mission and vision by describing why you decided to start it, and why now?

Try to present the facts about your message and business, like its establishment and vision, without making it seem like a resume. This is also not the place to be promotional. Save that for your product descriptions and other pages. A few things to include are:

➢ When and where did the transformative journey start?
➢ Who are you as a Messenger?
➢ Why is this the transformative journey they should embark on?
➢ Describe your mission, vision, and values.
➢ With social proof, show how you've helped others, and how you can help them.
➢ Present little-known or interesting facts about you and your journey.

Answer these questions from the point of view of your potential tribe members. Try to imagine what they're asking themselves as they look at your About Page. Speak in a tone that's relatable to your tribe members.

Identify the bit of your content that will be most important to your tribe members and organize your About Page so that the most important information is at the top. For example, if you want to emphasize that your coaching practice is more geared to single mothers in their 30's versus older women with adult children then this should be made clear from the onset.

If your mission is what most appeals to your audience, put this front and center. For example, you might have a strong commitment to health and wellness and everything you do is based on that view, make your position plain.

Since your About Us page should be personal, it's good to include graphics or pictures of you, your work, and settings where you serve. The real and authentic face of a real person gives any webpage a distinctly human touch. Take a real picture of you and others in your organization. Don't simply use a stock image. Adding different types of media also makes it more interesting for the visitor. Videos are great too, but don't make your About Page only a video.

Include social media links and update this page regularly with news and updates about your journey and what they can learn with you. Make sure all of the information here is relevant and interesting.

Don't make your About Page only about you. Use it to describe how you help people and what offers speak to that. Good About Pages are not about "me," but **"you and me."**

Further Tips on About Us Page Content

Like your Home Page, be sure to use SEO keywords on your About Page. People will also find this page through internet search. Use your name often as well, but naturally.

Be concise. Don't make your About Page wordy or disorganized. Present the information in a way that's quick and clear so that it's easy for the potential tribe member to understand.

Add a contact link from the About Page. Be ready to answer inquiries from visitors there who have further questions.

Here is a link to see some great About Us pages:

www.michaelhyatt.com/about

www.caesarkalinowski.com/about/

Designing Your Awesome About Us Page

1. Define what story you want to tell about your company. List your mission, goals, and product benefits.

Your Story

Your Mission

Your Goals

Benefits of Product & Services

2. Examine your current About Page and using the provided About Page template, fill in the information that needs to be added or edited from your page.

About Page Template

(You don't need all of these elements *and the order in which you place* them is up to you):

Your Story & History:	
Mission and Values:	
What Makes You Unique:	
Your Team:	

Social Media Links:	
Tribe Member Testimonials:	

Contact Link:	
Links to More Information (it's good to link to your Start Here page):	
Notable Recognition and Logos:	
A Bit of Personal Information (for website that are a personal brand, in particular)	

Compose Your Start Here Page

Your Start Page, or Welcome Page, is the portal to everything else your website has to offer. It gets first-time visitors started on the path which will lead them to your end goal. It assists them in finding the information they're looking for in a way that's quick and easy. The main purpose is to state who you are and to connect your potential tribe member with the next page they should visit on your website.

Start Page Content Must-Haves

Clarity – Since the goal is to make navigating your site easier, your Start Here page must have clarity. It should welcome the potential tribe member and tell them clearly that this is the page for getting started, and where to go next.

Your Objectives – Your Start Here page should state the objectives of your website in order to tell the visitor what they can expect. For example, if you're promoting courses, tell the potential tribe member that this is their one-stop shop for what you're offering. Tell them how they can use your website and emphasize its unique benefits.

Your Target – The Start Here page should not only set expectations, but also describe who this website is for. Your website is not for everyone, and the potential tribe member needs to know whether it's for them or not at the outset. It may seem like you're losing visitors by weeding them out in this way, but the people you'll lose would've left eventually when they figured out that it wasn't for them.

About Your Potential Tribe Member (Visitor) – Like your About Page, make it all about the potential tribe member. Even if you mention your offer or your services, ultimately focus on the benefit for the potential tribe member. Describe how it helps them, being careful not to spend too much time on specific products or services.

Logical Organization – Make your Start Here flow logically and naturally. Lead the visitor to the pages or information they're looking for. You can put it into a logical order by putting yourself in the shoes of your potential tribe member. What information are you looking for first, next, and so on? Imagine it as a flow chart that leads the potential tribe member to the action they need to take in order to realize their goal for visiting the site.

Call to Action – Now that you have provided the visitor with basic information, tell them what they need to do in order to get what they came to your site looking for. You can frame the action as what to do next; for example, "Check out our blog," "Sign up here," "Have a look at our product catalog," and so on.

Tips for Creating an Effective Start Here Page

Feel free to put multimedia on your Start Here Page as well as the other pages. An introductory video is good here but you should also have text content to help new visitors navigate your site.

You can also put social proof here, although it's not necessary. Testimonials and reviews work well on the sidebar of the Start Here page. Make sure they don't distract from the main purpose of the page, which is to provide navigation help.

Many sites use the Start Here page as a place to show off their best content. You can put links here to your most popular or most useful blog posts, articles, and other content.

Be careful to not duplicate too much of what's on your About Page. The About Page is more factual and more focused on your offerings (but framed in terms of benefits to the potential tribe member). The Start Here page's sole function is to help visitors.

Here are a few links of good Start Here pages:

www.michaelhyatt.com/start-here

www.caesarkalinowski.com/start-here/

Composing Your Start Here Page

1. Using the provided outline, document what you need the user to understand so they will comfortably navigate to other pages on your website based on what they're looking for.

Here are questions to help you outline your Start Here page (you don't need to include everything):

Who is this site for?	
What is this page specifically for?	
What will your user gain from the site?	
Who are you?	
What can people expect?	
What is some of the most popular content for visitors to look at first?	
How can users find you?	
How can users contact you?	
What are your most popular or important services?	

List 3 Calls to Action that would benefit the customer and move them further along the sales cycle and engage them more on your website. Note where you will put the calls to action on your Start Here page.

Call To Action	Location

Build a Compelling Blog (That Keeps Tribe Members Coming Back)

The purpose of your Blog page is to provide content that will engage potential tribe members and get them to read more. This content builds your reputation for expertise in your field. You share your knowledge here, and this is evident to anyone who reads your blog.

Your blog also serves as a magnet for search engine traffic. By posting new content regularly, you'll bring more traffic to your site. It's also one more good point of contact you can have with your potential tribe members and site visitors.

What Is a Blog Page and Why Is It Important?

Your Blog page is the home page of your blog. It includes your most recent posts as well as an archive of posts that have come before. Visitors can browse through the latest entries or they can search for specific topics from the past.

Your Blog page is important for a couple of reasons. First, it serves as a repository for all of your knowledge and expertise in one place. You can direct people to your blog when they want to learn more about a specific topic, or use it to address topics that are commonly discussed.

The other important function your Blog page serves is that it allows your site to grow. You may make some changes or update other parts of your website as necessary, but there won't be major changes. However, your Blog page allows you to post fresh content regularly. The other pages are all about conciseness and keeping it short, but on your blog, you can go in-depth into topics that really matter to your visitors.

Another advantage is that your content, here on your blog and elsewhere as well, establishes you as a thought leader. You become an expert in your field, which helps to bring you more readers, more visitors, and ultimately more tribe members.

There are SEO benefits because when you add new content, you add content that Google and other search engines can index. You can write around good high-traffic keywords that will help to bring more search traffic to your site. You can also use your blog as part of your back-linking strategy by linking to products/services, your social media profiles, other sites, and more. In fact, you can promote your services directly through your blog.

Why You Might Not Want a Blog Page on Your Website

There are a few reasons why you might not want to add a blog to your website. One is that it's better to have no blog on your site than a bad blog. You may choose not to include a Blog page if:

➢ You can't update it regularly
➢ You can't write or don't have the resources to hire someone to write it for you
➢ Your blog offers nothing new or original
➢ The tone of your blog doesn't match the rest of your website
➢ Your blog is overly promotional

If one or more of the bullet points above applies to your blog, you may not want to include it, but it's better to invest in making the improvements necessary because of all of the advantages a Blog page offers.

Another reason you may not want a Blog page on your site is if your brand or company is maintaining a blog somewhere else. This other blog may already have brand recognition or a following, in which case you don't want to start from scratch. If it's already associated with your company, you may instead want to simply link your blog and website, rather than put a Blog page on the site.

Elements to Include on Your Blog Page

Your blog should have a title and a headline that clearly describe you and your blog. Visitors should be able to take this in at a glance. It's helpful if in some way it describes the benefits of reading your blog; for example, your headline might say something like, "The latest tips on (your topic) to help you succeed at (your visitors' goal)."

Somewhere on your Blog page, such as in the sidebar, there should be a profile of you or the writer of your blog (if it's someone within your organization). Go for the personal touch here and include an appropriate headshot of you or the writer. The bio should give some personal details and also explain the writer's expertise; in other words, why you should read the blog ("Bob has been running a successful plumbing and waterproofing business in southern New Jersey for 20 years").

Each post should have a call to action. If you don't include one, you're missing out on a great opportunity. Even if the call is to read more, check out the other pages of your website, or connect with you on social media, you should take advantage of this opportunity.

Create categories for your posts. For each post, choose to which category it will belong. Use tags as well. Tags make your posts searchable. Categories and tags make it easier for visitors to find the topics they're looking for.

One element you should consider is commenting. The advantage of commenting is that it allows your readers to get involved, and it also gives you a direct line of communication with them. The downside is that you have to moderate comments regularly. You may get negative comments, trolls, and spam.

There are some elements you might consider putting on your Blog page's side bar. These are good elements for the side bar because you don't want them to distract from the main part of your page, which is the blog content itself.

Things to include are:

➤ Social media buttons so that people can share your content easily
➤ "Join me on" social media links
➤ A subscription form for readers to subscribe to your blog
➤ More social proof in the form of reviews, testimonials, or social media activity
➤ Information on products and services
➤ A contact form where people can reach you directly from the Blog page

Your Blog Page Style Guide

With your blog, cover topics that are interesting to your visitors. If you're not sure what's interesting, conduct some research. Look at popular posts on blogs in the same niche. Consider commonly asked questions. Every question you've been asked by a customer is a great potential blog post topic. Look at forums and social media sites to see what people are talking about. Another idea is to write a commentary on some news story related to your industry.

Aside from purely informational content, you can also blog about your company, its people, and its products. Showcase a new product or write about a change in your company. Take the reader behind the scenes in how your company or industry works. It's good to write about your company some, but make most of the content informational.

Since one of the advantages of blogging is its SEO benefits, you should try your best to incorporate relevant keywords. Find high-traffic, relevant keywords that the visitors you want will be looking for. If possible, use these keywords in titles and headers. Use wherever you can but keep it natural.

Write using small paragraphs with headers to separate different topics within one post. The idea is to make sure the text isn't dense or too wordy. People are intimidated by huge chunks of text, especially on a computer screen where it can be difficult to read. Make the font big and choose colors that are easy on the eyes.

Here are a few links of nice blog pages:

www.chalenejohnson.com (click blog)

http://www.marieforleo.com/blog/

http://brendon.com/blog/

Creating your Compelling Blog

1. After reviewing the module, determine if you should have a blog page on your website and if you do, draft an outline of the components you'll include on the main Blog Page.

Components	Notes

2. If you already have a blog on your site, review it based on the guidelines in this module and note where you need to add or make changes.

Content that will engage and get visitors to read more	
Builds reputation for expertise	
Regular posting?	
Titles and headlines that are clear and descriptive	
Describes benefits of reading the blog	
Includes a profile of the writer	
Includes a Call to Action in each post	
Categories for every post	
Ability to comment (with your moderation)	
Some things to include on the sidebar:	
➢ Social media buttons	
➢ 'Join me on' social media links	

➤ Subscription form	
➤ Social proof/Testimonials	
➤ Information on products and services	
➤ Contact form	
Covers topics that are interesting to your visitors	
Addresses common questions	
Blog about your company or products/services	
Incorporates relevant keywords	
Uses keywords in titles and headers	
Small paragraphs with headers	
Uses large fonts and easy to read colors	

Additional Web Pages to Include

We've covered the main pages of your site, but that's not all that your site needs. There are a few other critical pages every website should have. These are basic and not all of them have a lot of content, but you should include them on your website if it's a business site.

Contact Us

Every site needs a Contact Us page. It can be very simple. The sole purpose is to give visitors an easy way to contact you directly from the site. Visitors may rarely ever use it, but simply having it there helps you to build trust. Even though you may rarely receive inquiries, be ready to respond.

The wording on your Contact Us page should be concise and professional. No flashy or impressive design elements are needed. For an even better Contact Us page, tell potential tribe members how long it will take for you to respond to their inquiry (and stick to it). For an excellent Contact Us page, consider adding an 800 number where visitors can call you.

Test your Contact Us page to make sure it works after you set it up and whenever you make any changes.

Site Map

A site map is like an index or directory that lists all of the pages on a website. It lists the pages in a hierarchical way that describes the basic structure and navigation.

Site maps aren't for visitors but for search engines. Adding a site map to your site offers serious SEO benefits because it basically tells the search engines how to index your site and what kind of content can be found here. In addition, a site map helps a new website get indexed more quickly.

Legal Requirements

You should have a page for all of the legal requirements of running your website. These requirements might include disclaimers, your privacy policy, licensing information, credentials, terms of use, guidelines for abuse or complaints, and so on.

The purpose is not only to inform but also to build trust. When a visitor looks at this page, they can see that you're doing everything in accordance with the law. The privacy policy, which states how you use a visitor's information, is especially important.

In some cases, such as advertising on Facebook, you may be required to have a page for this information on your website.

Help / FAQ

A help or FAQ page that answers common questions can be very helpful for your potential tribe members. Your visitors come to your site with questions on their mind. This page answers those questions and organizes this information so that it's easy to understand quickly.

Make this page simple, clear, and searchable. Brainstorm common questions your potential tribe members may have. Try to imagine the doubts in their mind and provide answers that settle these doubts. When you receive new questions, add them to this page. Organize the information so that the most common questions are answered closest to the top. Wherever possible, link to further information.

You can spice up your help or FAQ page by adding graphics or images wherever appropriate. Sometimes a graphic can answer a question in a very simple way. You can break questions up into categories. Another idea is to create a second page or section for "Not So Frequently Asked Questions."

404 Error Page

A 404 Error page lets a user know when an error has occurred and what to do next. It's very important to include this or you'll lose site visitors when an error occurs. The 404 Error page leads the user back to your website and prevents them from leaving. It's also a good way to point potential tribe members to popular content that you want them to see.

Business-Specific Web Pages

Here are some typical pages a business website would also include. These are optional pages. For each, you should consider whether this would help your website become more effective and user-friendly or not.

Products and Services

The Products and Services page lists your specific products and services and provides specific information about each one. However, its true underlying purpose is to help the potential tribe member make an informed buying decision when shopping from you. In addition to a catalog of your products and services, this page should tell the potential tribe members where and how to make their purchase from you. If you're selling through the site, include a link to your store where the user can make the actual final purchase.

Your Products and Services page should be organized based on what the visitor is looking for. Consider the source or page that's referring them here. Which information would be most useful at the top of the page?

Businesses usually put their newest or most popular products at the top of the page. Other products and services should be listed in a logical order and broken up into relevant categories where necessary. It's essential that your Products and Services page have search functionality so that potential tribe members can find products through keywords.

Each product or service should have a short, clear description. If you keep descriptions short, the potential tribe members can see more products or services on the page at once. When descriptions must be longer, break up the text into headers and sub-headers. For extended descriptions, include a link that expands the description or leads to a product page.

Descriptions should include features and benefits, pricing, materials used, and any warranties, certifications or licensing information that's relevant.

Testimonials are optional on your Products and Services page. You may choose to include a short testimonial in your extended product description.

Again, keep the Products and Services page focused on meeting the potential tribe member's needs and helping them make the right choice, rather than trying to sell your products. Remember, if they are looking through your products then they are already interested in buying from you, all you should be doing is helping them as much as possible in their decision-making process. Describe each feature and relate it to the potential tribe members by explaining the unique benefit your service or product offers. Organize listings so that the user is likely to find what they want quickly. Provide general buying information that your customers need to know in order to make their purchase.

Pricing

If you're offering a type of product or service where there's a set price, you can have a separate pricing page. The advantage to a page like this, rather than listing each price for each product, is that it's very easy for your visitor to understand without needing to browse your catalog.

For services or products where the basic product is the same but there are different plans, you should create a simple graphic that explains how the pricing works. Take special care to emphasize the specific features and benefits so that your potential tribe members can make their decision on this page. On this page, you should also include a link where the visitor can contact you directly. This is a page where potential tribe members are likely to have questions, so don't make them go back to your Contact Us page to ask.

On your Pricing page or Products and Services page, add some content that addresses any buying doubts or uncertainties. For example, if you have a free money-back guarantee, state this clearly. This will encourage the potential tribe member to buy from you.

Online Shop

An Online Shop is a page where the user can actually buy from you. It might be combined with your Products and Services or Pricing page (or all three may be put together).

The Online Shop has a shopping cart where the user makes their final purchase. There are many different shopping cart programs you can use. Whichever you decide to use, always test your Online Shop and shopping cart regularly to make sure it works smoothly. Choose one where there are the fewest steps involved before the final purchase.

The key to the content of your Online Shop is trustworthiness. Include links to your FAQ, content that quells doubts and uncertainties, and social proof and testimonials.

Site Search

It's good to include a site search on your website. This is usually not a page by itself but a menu bar on the Home Page or on the other page of your site. This makes your site more user-friendly and allows potential tribe members to find the key information they're looking for quickly. This can also increase the amount of time a visitor spends on your site, which offers SEO benefits as well. Google analyzes website visitor behavior and takes it into account when indexing sites. It can also directly increase your sales.

Testimonials / Reviews Page

We've discussed adding testimonials, reviews, and other social proof to various pages of your site in order to inspire trust and confidence. You can also create your own page for testimonials and social proof. If you want to build a separate page for social proof, decide how you'll integrate it into your overall site's structure. For example, you could put links to your social proof page on your Online Store page saying something like, "See what other people have said about our programs."

Opt-in Pages

An opt-in page is a page where visitors can submit their name and email to receive offers, news, and content from you by email. This is part of an email marketing strategy. It allows you to keep in touch with your potential tribe members, build a more personal relationship by communicating with them directly through email, and provide invitations to partner with you through exclusive offers.

Like social proof, you can either create a standalone page, or put your opt-in form various places on your site like the sidebar of your blog, or both.

The text of your Opt-in page should be compelling. It should tell the potential tribe members what they'll receive for signing up and emphasize the benefits for them. Emphasize that they'll receive exclusive content they can't get anywhere. The offer to sign up should be free and, in fact, you can increase sign-ups by offering a free download as incentive. This could be an eBook, video course, resource guide, podcast series, or anything else of value to your visitor.

Thank You Page

If you have an Opt-in page or form, you should also have a Thank You page. Once the visitor has signed up, they're redirected to this page, which thanks them for joining, reminds them of the benefits, offers additional free content, and/or optionally upsells them by making another offer. You can also provide coupons, discounts, or other ways to increase your business here.

Press / News

You may want to add a site with press or news in the media about your business. This continues to build trust and helps to build a relationship. It also lets visitors know what's new with your business. In addition to content from third party media outlets, you can also post your own press releases here that announce when there's something new. Adding fresh content here, like your blog, helps increase your exposure with search engines.

Events

If you're actively participating in or hosting events, create an Events page to tell your potential tribe members all about it. This is a great link to share on your social media stream or elsewhere whenever a new event is added or updated. You can also include events you're attending, events you like, events related to your products, or events where your product are being used. Any event connected with your business can be announced here and it helps to promote your business.

Resources

One final page you should consider is a Resources page. This links to sponsors or other sites that help visitors with further information. Things you can include along with purely informational resources include your downloads, articles published elsewhere, news articles, or additional product information.

Additional Web Pages to Include

1. List the additional "Must Have" web pages for your own website, based on the needs of your business, and a brief summary of what you would include in each.

2. List the Business-Specific web pages needed for your site and what you will need to add or edit from what you learned in this module.

	Must-Have Pages	Summary
1	Contact Us	
2	Site Map	
3	Legal Requirements	
4	Help/FAQ	
5	404 Error Page	

	Business-Specific Pages	Summary
6	Products and Services	
7	Pricing	
8	Online Shop	
9	Site Search	
10	Testimonials/Reviews	
11	Opt In Pages	
12	Thank You Page	
13	Press/News	
14	Events	
15	Resources	

Best Practices When Curating Content

Design Considerations

One major factor contributing to whether your content is read and thus the effectiveness of your website is its design. Enhancing and improving the design can help to create a better user experience and thus improve your site's performance. A few considerations here include:

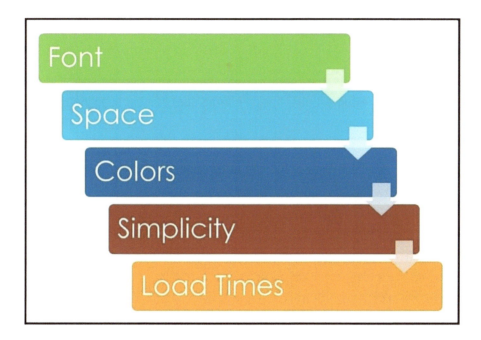

- ➢ **Font:** Is the font unique and consistent with your brand? Is it easy to read? What does the font say about you?
- ➢ **Space:** Make sure there's plenty of white space and avoid large chunks of text. White space also helps to create balance. It also accentuates features like your call to action.
- ➢ **Colors:** Use a font color and background color that makes it easy to read. Avoid dark background with light text, and avoid stark black and white; use greyscale instead for better readability.
- ➢ **Simplicity:** Keep the design simple. It's better for it to be too clean than too cluttered.
- ➢ **Load Times:** Don't use any design elements that take a long time to load, like Flash players. Users may not stay and wait.
- ➢ **Mobile-Friendly:** Design your pages so that they're mobile-friendly or mobile-responsive, or create a separate mobile version of your site.

Content Tips

The quality of your content is critical to building relationships with your customers. It really has to be exceptional. If your web pages are full of generic or poorly written content, it doesn't matter how well you've planned. Your website won't achieve its goals.

Good content is unique and high-quality. It offers a distinctive take on the subject and gives the reader information that they can use. While being informative, it is also interesting, entertaining and easy to read. Take a look at the website you frequently read and ask yourself why you read them.

If you're not confident about writing your own content, hire a ghost writer. Take time and find someone who knows the subject matter well, is reliable and writes well. Try to choose just one or a handful of good writers with whom you can build a close, long-term relationship. Don't choose a writer based on price alone.

Making Your Site Search-Friendly

There are many things you can do to make your website easy for search engines to find and index. We've covered some of them already. Here are some further tips on making sure that the search engines find your content and send users to it.

➢ **Keywords**. We've covered this already, but find some good keywords and use them naturally wherever possible. Choose the type of keywords your ideal customer would be searching for. Update the keywords you use or change them up from time to time.

➢ **Uniqueness**. All of your content needs to be unique. Don't copy and paste content from elsewhere. You should use only content that's original because search engine algorithms index content only once; if your content is copied from somewhere else, it won't show up in search results.

➢ **Inbound Links.** Invite others to link back to you and actively look for sites that will give you a quality backlink. It's important that these are "quality" backlinks, not just links from random sites that you've paid for.

Best Practices When Curating Content

1. Based on the tips in this module, review your current site and document what best practices you will revisit to enhance the overall content and design of the key pages on your website.

Consider:	
➢ Font	
➢ Space	
➢ Colors	
➢ Simplicity	
➢ Load Times	
➢ Mobile-Friendly	
Content quality	
Keywords	
Uniqueness	
Inbound Links	

Conclusion

When designing your website, always keep in mind your potential tribe member's experience. This is what gets people to stay on your site and it's also what search engines look for. If your site offers a good user experience, which includes easy site navigation and useful content, it will keep potential tribe members coming back for more. This is how you strengthen your relationship with your ideal tribe members.

Once you've built your website, check to make sure that it supports your ministry/business goals and objectives. Once your new and improved website goes live, is it attracting the new leads it's supposed to? If not, what changes do you need to make? Let your analytics guide you in deciding.

Once you have your site and its pages set up, keep updating it with fresh content that meets your tribe member's needs. Always keep your ears open and keep the lines of communication strong so that you can get feedback and learn exactly what they need and want from you. Think of your website as a means of answering your ideal tribe member's questions.

In this self-study course, you have learned:

➢ The key pages your website needs and the specific purpose of each
➢ The essential elements of an effective Home page and how to create them for your website
➢ The components needed to create a compelling and effective About Us page that tells your story and answers initial visitor questions
➢ How to create a Start Here page that will effectively guide your potential tribe members to the action you want them to take
➢ How to create a Blog page and keep it updated with fresh content
➢ The other web pages that are essential to a business website, as well as a list of optional web pages you may want to incorporate
➢ Best practices and tips for maintaining a successful website
➢ How to put your ideas into action by utilizing the planning templates

Now, you're ready to put your plan into action. Be sure to include a deadline with each task you need to carry out. Keep in mind that creating a great website isn't something you do just once. It requires regular monitoring and maintaining. But if done well, it can very effectively bring potential tribe members to your business.

Conclusion

1. Review your notes and what you have learned so far.

2. Identify 5 ways you can enhance your current website or what is needed for your new one.

1	
2	
3	
4	
5	

3. Review your work from previous modules and prioritize the changes you will make once you get back to work.

Write them below:

4. Write down the tasks and timelines you will do as soon as you get back to work.

Task	Notes	Deadline

APPENDIX

Web Content – Summary Checklist

Introduction –Key Pages for Your Website

- ✓ The key question is 'What do you want your potential tribe members to do?'
- ✓ Start with your end goal in mind
- ✓ You need to clarify:
  - o Who are you?
  - o What are you offering?
  - o What call to action do you want to create?
  - o Where did your potential tribe member come from?
  - o What does your potential tribe member need?
- ✓ You can segment your site according to potential tribe member groups
- ✓ You can organize by topic
- ✓ You can organize according to where they have come from
- ✓ Prioritize content and decide where it goes

- ✓ **This course focused on:**
  - o Home Page
  - o About Us
  - o Start Here Page
  - o Blog Page
  - o Other pages that may be needed according to site type

- ✓ **You've learned:**
  - o Key pages you need
  - o How to identify and incorporate the most important components
  - o How to produce an About Us page that tells your story
  - o The importance of the Start Here page
  - o The value of a well-designed Blog page
  - o Other pages you need
  - o Best practices
  - o How to create a personalized action plan

Create an Impeccable Home Page

- ✓ Your home page tells potential tribe members who you are, what you do and what you have to offer
- ✓ It should address questions and problems
- ✓ Show solutions
- ✓ Start with the goal you have in mind for the site
- ✓ Put yourself in your potential tribe members shoes
  - o Who is this?
  - o What do they do?
  - o Who do they serve?
  - o What makes them different?
  - o What else do they have to offer?
- ✓ Content should answer these basic questions

Elements of a Good Home Page

- ✓ It's compelling and makes potential tribe members want to stay and interact
- ✓ It's clear and speaks to expectations
- ✓ It is well organized and easy to take in
- ✓ Navigation is clear
- ✓ It should be dynamic and include news and updates
- ✓ Fresh content also helps with SEO

The Essential Components of a Good Home Page

- ✓ Your Home Page should include:
  - o A headline
  - o Visuals
  - o Bullet-point list of benefits
  - o Call to Action
  - o Introduction to other pages

Additional Optional Components for Your Home Page

- ✓ Content Offer
  - o Some kind of freebie to download
- ✓ Social Proof
  - o Testimonials or reviews

Content Tips for Your Home Page

- ✓ Content should be brief
- ✓ Make it personal to connect with the reader
- ✓ Break up text into small paragraphs
- ✓ Use keywords in a natural way
- ✓ Always proofread all content
- ✓ Make a good first impression

Design Your Awesome About Us Page

- ✓ The About Us page starts building a relationship with potential tribe members
- ✓ They're looking for information and similar values
- ✓ Along with the Home page, it's the most visited page

Creating Your About Page Content

- ✓ Tell the potential tribe member about you
- ✓ Make it personal and tell a story
- ✓ Don't get into product or service specifics
- ✓ Present facts about your business but don't be promotional
- ✓ Some things to include:
  - o When/where did the message/business start?
  - o Why you do what you do?
- ✓ Answer questions from the potential tribe members point of view
- ✓ Place the most important information at the top
- ✓ Include (real) graphics or pictures
- ✓ Include social media links
- ✓ Update news regularly
- ✓ Make sure all info is relevant and interesting

Further Tips on About Us Page Content

- ✓ Use SEO Keywords
- ✓ Be concise
- ✓ Add a contact link

Begin with Your Start Here Page

- ✓ Your Start Page is the portal to everything else your site has to offer
- ✓ It will lead visitors to your end goal

✓ The main purpose is to state who you are and to connect your visitor with the page they need

Start Page Content Must-Haves

✓ Clarity
  ○ It should welcome and clearly tell people where to go
✓ Your Objectives
  ○ Tell visitors what to expect
✓ Your Target
  ○ Set expectations and describe who the site is for
✓ About Your Visitor
  ○ Make it all about the visitor
✓ Logical Organization
  ○ Make it flow logically and naturally
✓ Call to Action
  ○ Tell them what they need to do

Tips for Creating an Effective Start Here Page

✓ Use multimedia, like an introductory video
✓ Use social proof
✓ Show off your best content
✓ Don't duplicate too much from the About Us page
✓ The sole function is to help visitors

Create a Compelling Blog that Keeps Tribe Members Coming Back

✓ Provide content that will engage and get potential tribe members to read more
✓ Build reputation for expertise
✓ Regular posting will bring more traffic to your site

What is a Blog Page and Why is it Important?

✓ Most recent and archived posts
✓ Serves as a repository for all of your knowledge and expertise
✓ Allows your site to grow
✓ Establish yourself as a thought leader through content
✓ SEO benefits
✓ Use as part of your back-linking strategy

Why You Might Not Want a Blog Page on Your Website

- ✓ Better to have no blog than a bad blog
- ✓ Reasons for no blog include:
  - o You can't update regularly
  - o You can't write it
  - o It doesn't offer anything new or original
  - o The tone doesn't match the site, It's overly promotional
- ✓ You may maintain a blog elsewhere

Elements to Include on Your Blog Page

- ✓ It should have a title and headline that is clear and descriptive
- ✓ Describe benefits of reading the blog
- ✓ Include a profile of the writer
- ✓ Include a Call to Action in each post
- ✓ Create categories for posts
- ✓ Commenting allows readers to get involved, but has to be moderated
- ✓ Some things to include on the sidebar are:
  - o Social media buttons
  - o 'Join me on' social media links
  - o Subscription form
  - o Social proof/Testimonials
  - o Information on products and services
  - o Contact form

Your Blog Page Style Guide

- ✓ Cover topics that are interesting to your visitors
- ✓ Consider common questions
- ✓ Blog about your services and transformation you offer
- ✓ Incorporate relevant keywords
- ✓ Use keywords in titles and headers
- ✓ Write small paragraphs with headers
- ✓ Use large fonts and easy to read colors

Additional Critical Website Pages to Include

There are a few other critical pages every site should have, particularly business sites.

Contact Us

- ✓ Sole purpose is to give an easy way to contact you
- ✓ Having it there builds trust
- ✓ Be ready to respond
- ✓ Wording should be concise and professional
- ✓ Tell potential tribe members how long it will take you to respond
- ✓ Test your page and make sure it works

Site Map

- ✓ An index or directory that lists all of the pages
- ✓ Describes basic structure and navigation
- ✓ Offers great SEO benefits

Legal Requirements

- ✓ Disclaimers, Privacy policy, licensing info, credentials, terms of use, etc
- ✓ Inform and build trust
- ✓ You may be required to have this information for things like advertising

Help/FAQ

- ✓ Answer questions and organize information
- ✓ Make it simple, clear and searchable
- ✓ Brainstorm common questions
- ✓ Add graphics or images
- ✓ Add 'Not So Frequently Asked Questions'

404 Error Page

- ✓ Let a visitor know an error has occurred and what to do
- ✓ Lead the user back to your site
- ✓ Prevent them from leaving

Business-Specific Web Pages

- ✓ Optional pages
- ✓ Would it help your site or not?
- ✓ Products and Services
  - o List and information
  - o Help buying decisions

- o Consider structure and layout
- o Keep descriptions short and clear
- o Features, benefits & testimonials
- ✓ Pricing
  - o When you're offering a type of product or service with a set price
  - o Easy to understand
  - o For different plans, create a graphic to explain pricing
  - o Emphasize features and benefits
  - o Add a comparison chart
- ✓ Online shop
  - o Where a potential tribe member can actually buy from you
  - o Shopping cart
  - o Choose one with the fewest stops
  - o Include links to FAQs and social proof
- ✓ Site Search
  - o Not an actual page
  - o Menu bar
  - o Makes the site more user-friendly
  - o Increase interaction
- ✓ Testimonials/Review Page
  - o You can create your own page for social proof
  - o Decide how you'll integrate it
  - o 'See what other people have said about us'
- ✓ Opt-In Pages
  - o Visitors submit their name and email
  - o Receive transformational offers, news and content
  - o Keep in touch and build relationships
  - o Create a standalone page or integrate a form
  - o Text should be compelling
  - o Sign up should be free and offer an incentive
- ✓ Thank You Page
  - o Once the visitor has signed up, they're directed here
  - o Thank them, remind them of benefits and make transformational offers
  - o Provide coupons/discounts/other ways for them to access you
- ✓ Press/News
  - o Continue to build trust and relationships
  - o Let visitors know what's new
  - o Fresh content helps exposure with search engines

- ✓ Events
    - ○ Create an events page to tell visitors what's going on
    - ○ Share on social media or elsewhere
    - ○ Include events you're attending or that are related
    - ○ Any event connected to your business can be announced
- ✓ Resources
    - ○ Links to sponsors or other sites for further info
    - ○ Downloads, articles, news, additional product info

Best Practices to Consider When Writing Your Website Content

Design Considerations

- ✓ Enhancing design can create a better experience
- ✓ Consider:
    - ○ Font
    - ○ Space
    - ○ Colors
    - ○ Simplicity
    - ○ Load Times
    - ○ Mobile-Friendly

Content Tips

- ✓ Content quality is critical to building relationships
- ✓ Bad content won't achieve goals
- ✓ Good content is unique and high-quality
- ✓ You can hire a ghost writer
- ✓ Find someone who knows the subject matter well
- ✓ Don't choose a writer based on price alone

Making Your Site Search Friendly

- ✓ Keywords
    - ○ Find good keywords and use them naturally
- ✓ Uniqueness
    - ○ Don't copy content from elsewhere
- ✓ Inbound Links
    - ○ Invite others to link back to you

Conclusion

- ✓ Keep your tribe member's experience in mind.
- ✓ (This will keep them coming back to experience more.)
- ✓ Check that your site is aligned with your tribal goals and objectives
- ✓ Keep updating your site with fresh insights and transformative content
- ✓ Keep your ears open and learn from feedback
- ✓ Think of your site as a means of transforming your tribe member's lives
- ✓ You have learned:
  - o Key pages and the purpose of each
  - o Essential elements of an effective homepage
  - o Components of a compelling about us page
  - o How to create a Start Here page to guide visitors
  - o How to create an update a blog page
  - o Other essential pages
  - o Best practices
  - o How to put ideas into action
- ✓ Now put your plan into action with deadlines
- ✓ Remember creating a good website requires monitoring and maintaining

Creating Your Ideal Tribe Member Profile

Insights gleaned from this process will inspire your communications and spark ideas to enhance your messaging, offerings, and services. This questionnaire should be completed for every new product, service or offering you create.

Now let's step in their shoes...

Introducing...

Name:

Age/Gender:

Marital Status/Children (if applicable)/(Include Names):

Where do they live?:

Income:

Occupation/Parent's Occupation:

How does she see and feel about herself?

Life Beliefs:

Favorite Books, Music, TV Shows:

Magazines/Articles she reads:

What does she Google? (List her concerns/interests):

Now BE your clan or tribe member. This is about feeling and emotion. Step into their skin. Look at life through their eyes.

What primary emotion, or set of emotions, does she feel when she's interacting with your messaging, or is about to buy your product or services?

What is she saying to herself in her head? What specific words and phrases is she using? What story is she telling herself?

It's time to go deep and be specific. Answer the following questions as your ideal tribe member. You need to answer these questions with honesty and candor.

What do you secretly fear may be true about your situation?

What do you worry about? What keeps you up at night?

What do you **not** look at because it triggers too much fear or pain?

How do you fear others (close friends, family, spouse, clients) would react if they found out about your situation?

What do you fear might fail in your life if your situation continues or if it gets worse?

What do you secretly wish was true about your situation?

What do you hope is actually true about your situation?

What is their **"oh my, I can't believe this exists"** ('dream solution') that you'd do anything to be a part of?"

About your Course Facilitator

Terikka Faciane has been uniquely commissioned as a midwife to Messengers. She is passionately committed to helping transformational leaders clarify, refine, and birth their God-given message so they can effectively reach their tribe. Her aim is to ensure excellence and preparedness in guiding each transformational leader entrusted to her care towards the fulfillment of sharing their life's message.

To guide messengers on this clarifying journey, Terikka has tirelessly honed and refined the identity, vision, and messaging awareness processes for almost 2 decades now, and continues to do so.

Regardless of the hustle-and-bustle of the surroundings in which you may chance upon her, whether it be at one of her high-octane destiny awareness workshops or just an enthusiastic introduction made by one of her satisfied tribe members; you will hear Terikka pose the question, "So, what are you passionate about?" – And once engaged in conversation, you will leave with the impression that "It's Time" for your life to take on a dramatically different tone. You will know your life was meant to speak and there is someone waiting and needing to hear what only your life has to say.

Upon initial interaction with Terikka, one cannot help but feel justified in the conviction that "there is more to my existence than this." Terikka has been sent to show you the Self, the Messenger, you were meant to become. Armed with an infectious enthusiasm, a life-affirming message of her own, her flexible coaching (midwifing) style adapts to the evolution of her tribe member's needs. With an arsenal of clarifying tools, resources, and interactive exercises that act as illuminating signposts; Terikka is fully equipped to get you moving—and keep you moving—on your unique path to becoming the Messenger God has called you to be.

Think of her presentations, guided resources, books, mastermind alliances, and self-study courses as a 'reunion-esque" introduction she's strategically facilitating between you, your truest self, and the tribe you have been called to reach; where one can almost envision Terikka saying, with encouragement and conviction, "It's Time, your tribe is waiting for you!"

EDUCATION:

- Doctorate in Leadership for Educational Justice, TBD (All Coursework Completed) University of Redlands, Redlands, CA
- Masters of Arts, Education with an emphasis in School Counseling, August 2005, University of Redlands, Redlands, CA
- Pupil Personnel Services Credential, August 2005, University of Redlands, Redlands, CA
- Bachelor of Arts, Biblical Studies, December 1999, Scholars Bible College, Moreno Valley, CA
- Bachelor of Arts, Psychology and Black Studies, May 1997, Pitzer College, a Member of the Claremont Colleges, Claremont, CA

To learn more about **The Messenger Experience**

or to find more Messenger resources, please visit

www.yourtribeiswaiting.com

www.ingramcontent.com/pod-product-compliance
Lightning Source LLC
Chambersburg PA
CBHW041431050326

40690CB00002B/505